FROM ZERO TO SIX FIGURES

A Lawyer's Journey — How I Built a

Six-Figure Practice in Six Months

CANDICE E. IHEME

Candice E. Iheme, Esq.

Candice@IhemeLegal.com

ISBN: 978-1-966840-21-3

Rest in peace, Eze Iheme. May I always make you proud.

Acknowledgments

I want to thank God, my husband, my mom, stepdad, uncles, sisters, friends, and all of my loved ones. Without you, I am incomplete. To my father in Heaven, please continue to watch over me.

DISCLAIMER

The strategies, insights, and advice shared in this book are based on my personal experiences and professional journey in building a successful law firm and business. It's important to note that when I started my firm, I already had a client base established with over 20 clients.

Many of my clients chose to continue working with me as I started my new firm. This book provides general guidance and best practices, but results may vary depending on individual circumstances, market conditions, and the nature of your business (i.e. your practice area and whether it is in high demand).

The information provided is for educational purposes only and should not be construed as legal, financial, or business advice tailored to your specific situation. I recommend consulting with professionals who can provide personalized advice based on your unique needs and goals.

CONTENTS

INTRODUCTION

- *"You have to be odd to be number one." — Dr. Seuss*

Success. It's a word that evokes a myriad of emotions—excitement, curiosity, even trepidation. But what if I told you that success is within your grasp, no matter where you're starting from? What does it take to turn a simple idea into a thriving six-figure business in just six months? Is it a matter of luck, timing, or something more?

If you've ever wondered how to scale your business rapidly and effectively, you're in the right place. This book is your guide to making it happen. As Peter Drucker famously said, "The best way to predict the future is to create it," and that philosophy is at the heart of this book. Whether you're an aspiring entrepreneur, a seasoned professional, or simply curious about the journey to success, this book is for you.

My name is Candice EgoEze Iheme , and I'm a first-generation American who found a career that ignited my passion for helping others and for entrepreneurship. My passion for community service began as a middle schooler when I was chosen to lead the Martin Luther King Jr. Club, which was dedicated to community service. My path to success contained many unexpected opportunities to lead, which pushed me to step up and grow in ways that I would have never imagined.

In 2015, while I was still in college, I began working for a Fortune 500 insurance company. When the job was first offered to me, I thought it would be extremely boring. Let's be honest: insurance? Who thinks that would be interesting? But it turns out, it was simply fascinating. My experience there is what led me to become an attorney.

I never planned to attend law school, but life has a funny way of leading you to your true calling. The more I immersed myself in the insurance world, the more I realized the critical role that knowledge plays in empowering individuals. Most people have insurance. Most people do not know what is and is not covered by their insurance (until it is too late, that is). I saw firsthand how many clients were unaware of the insurance benefits that they were legally entitled to. This inspired me to become an advocate for those who could not properly advocate for themselves.

I graduated *cum laude* from Rutgers University-New Brunswick with a bachelor's in economics and a minor in psychology. At the time, I did not realize how understanding both areas would help me as an attorney. I graduated with a full-time offer from that Fortune 500 insurance company. This offer included benefits, a pension, and the likelihood that

I would eventually become part of leadership within my office because I was a former intern.

I could have easily stayed at that insurance company and quickly scaled the corporate ladder into management. Yet, my growing awareness of the large disparity in power between these mega-corporations and average people pushed me toward a different destiny. I hated how my relationship with clients would end so prematurely. I also hated not being able to tell them when they were being lowballed and that, with the right attorney, they could recover so much more. During my time in insurance, I got to shadow their in-house attorneys and even go to court with them. All of these experiences compelled me to consider going to law school.

I began studying for the LSAT, scheduled the exam, took it, applied to one law school, and ended up attending Rutgers Law School in Newark. My time there was transformative. There were so many pathways to success in the law. Many people start law school having a goal in mind and then end up working in a completely different place than they had originally anticipated.

During law school, I served as a graduate resident assistant, chair of the Moot Court Board, LexisNexis research assistant, and clinical law student with the Rutgers Education and Health Law Clinic. I also interned at the District Court for the District of New Jersey, and in the New Jersey Superior Court, within the Criminal Division. I immersed myself in a world where law intersected with service. But I also got to experience interning at very reputable law firms[1]. By the time I graduated, I had a full-time offer from an AMLaw 100 law firm and an appointment to work as a law clerk in the Superior Court of New Jersey. Additionally, I had

---

[1] I got an offer to work as a legal intern at the insurance company for all three years including an offer to join them as in-house counsel upon graduation. A wise mentor told me to choose the scary option and work at a law firm so that I could gain more experience in different areas of the law. I am glad I took that risk because I learned so much in such a short amount of time. I was also able to network and meet many brilliant attorneys, whom I am still in touch with today. Growth does not always happen in your comfort zone!

accumulated over 600 pro bono hours assisting indigent families with children who had special needs. My mission was already clear: to fight for justice and make a tangible difference in the lives of people within my community. But how could I do so while working at a corporate law firm? Luckily, I had a whole year to figure that out while I clerked.

During my clerkship at one of New Jersey's busiest courts, I worked directly under a superior court judge. There, I was exposed to a wide range of legal issues, deepening my understanding of the intricacies of law.

Though I worked in the Criminal Division, I routinely volunteered to help other courts and in other divisions. This helped me learn even more. I handled several mediations in landlord-tenant court, volunteered to help in special civil, and assisted other criminal courts with cleaning up their dockets. I ran toward opportunities others ran away from, and I am a better lawyer because of it.

This experience I gained as a judicial law clerk was invaluable, providing a solid foundation for my career. I would not be where I am and would not have had this career trajectory without my judge. I then transitioned to an AMLaw100 Firm's Litigation Department before joining a boutique firm specializing in personal injury. It was here that I found my true calling—to advocate for the rights of individuals within the insurance world, but this time from the other side of the table.

At this moment, it felt as though my journey had come full circle. I left the insurance world to educate people about what they were entitled to. Now I got to go up against the "big dogs" and help even out the large disparity in power between these billion-dollar corporations and the average day people.

Today, I run my own law firm, handling a mix of personal injury, workers' compensation, and criminal defense cases. In just six months, I transformed this practice into a six-figure business.

The journey was filled with lessons, challenges, and triumphs. It is these experiences that I am eager to share with you. This book is not just a recounting of legal battles and business strategies; it's a blueprint for building a successful practice—or any business—grounded in ethical principles, strategic thinking, and a commitment to service.

The purpose of this book is to provide a comprehensive roadmap for scaling your business quickly and sustainably. Whether you're starting from scratch or looking to grow an existing practice, the strategies I share here are designed to be practical and actionable.

From identifying a niche to building a brand, mastering client relations, and leveraging technology and your network, this book covers several aspects of business growth. But beyond the mechanics, it's also about personal growth—developing the resilience, confidence, and vision needed to lead a successful enterprise. To lead a law firm, you cannot only be a good lawyer, **you must**

be a good business person. Talent is not enough; you must have business acumen.

This book is for lawyers who want to transform their practice into a thriving business. It's for entrepreneurs looking to scale their ventures rapidly. It's for anyone who believes in the power of hard work, smart strategies, and a passion for making a difference. This book is for those who want to learn from someone who has been in the trenches, faced the challenges, and emerged stronger and more successful.

By reading this book, you'll gain more than just business insights. You'll discover the power of perseverance, the importance of purpose, and the value of service. You'll learn how to navigate the legal landscape while building a business that aligns with your values and goals. Practical tips for managing your time, resources, and energy are woven throughout, ensuring that you don't just achieve financial success but also maintain a healthy work-life balance.

In the following chapters, I'll share the blueprint that helped me achieve rapid business growth. From developing a compelling value proposition to mastering the art of networking, the important aspects of building a successful business is covered. You'll find case studies, personal anecdotes, and actionable exercises designed to help you implement what you learn. This is not just a book to read; it's a guide to take action with.

As we embark on this journey together, I encourage you to have an open mind and a willingness to learn. The road to success is rarely straight, but with the right tools and mindset, you can navigate the twists and turns with confidence. Remember, the goal isn't just to build a business; it's to create a legacy, make an impact, and live a life that aligns with your highest values.

The path to entrepreneurship is often paved with challenges, but it is also filled with opportunities for growth and discovery. Taking a leap of faith is scary, but most people who do so never regret it.

My journey is a testament to the power of intention, affirmations, hard work, and strategic thinking. It's proof that with the right approach, anyone can achieve greatness. Whether you're a budding entrepreneur, a seasoned professional looking to pivot, or someone curious about what it takes to succeed, this book offers valuable insights and guidance.

As you read, you'll encounter practical insights and thought-provoking questions designed to challenge your assumptions and inspire action. Have you ever considered how your personal values align with your business goals? How do you balance ambition with ethics? These are the kinds of questions that will guide you toward a more intentional and fulfilling entrepreneurial journey. This book isn't just about making money; it's about making a difference, both in your life and in the lives of those you serve.

The stakes are high in the world of law and business, but so are the rewards. With the right tools and mindset, you can carve out a space for yourself, even in the most competitive industries. But this book isn't just about my story; it's about empowering you to create your own success story. By the end of this book, I want you to feel confident, inspired, and equipped with the knowledge to take your business to new heights.

You do not have to hate your job or your life. You can live a fantastic life and enjoy the work that you do. I am finally in a place where all of my hard work feels like it was worth it. I love it here. Everything is not perfect, but I am cultivating an environment that suits me. As an entrepreneur, I feel I am finally where I should be. I created this book so that others can feel the same.

So, are you ready to embark on this journey with me? Are you prepared to break through the barriers that hold you back and step into a world of unlimited potential? Together, we'll explore the strategies, mindsets, and actions necessary to build a business that not only succeeds but thrives.

Let this book be your guide, your mentor, and your source of inspiration as you navigate the exciting world of entrepreneurship. The road ahead may be challenging, but it's also filled with endless opportunities. And remember, the journey is just as important as the destination.

As you read, keep an open mind and a curious heart. The knowledge you'll gain here is not just theoretical; it's practical, tested, and proven. It's the same knowledge that helped me transform my law firm into a six-figure powerhouse in just six months (and this is only the beginning; the sky isn't the limit). And if I can do it, so can you. This book is your invitation to step into a future of success and fulfillment. Let's go!

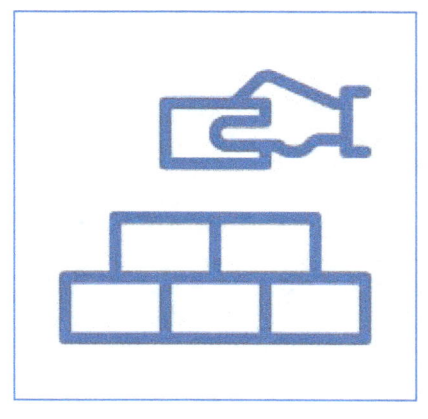

PART I :

FOUNDATIONAL STEPS

CHAPTER 1

Building Your Legal Foundation

- *"Those who step out on faith, rarely regret it."*
  — *Candice Sodeinde*

Starting your own business, whether it's a law firm or any other venture, is one of the most exciting and challenging things you can do. I remember when I first decided to start my own practice—I was full of ambition but also fully aware that building the foundation correctly was critical. Building a business is like building a house. You wouldn't build a house on shaky ground, and you certainly wouldn't skip laying a solid foundation. The same principle applies to your business. The decisions you make early on, from the business structure to the name, will have long-lasting effects on your success.

In this chapter, we'll dive deep into the essential steps for establishing a solid foundation for your business. We'll explore the critical choices you'll face, like selecting the right business structure, understanding the legal and ethical considerations of naming your business, and the importance of consulting with professionals to ensure compliance and protection. These aren't just formalities; they're strategic decisions that will shape your business's future.

Choosing the Right Business Structure

When I first started thinking about starting my own law firm, one of the most important decisions I faced was choosing the right business structure. But this isn't just a law firm issue—every entrepreneur needs to make this decision, and it's one that will impact everything, from how you operate daily to how you pay taxes, protect your personal assets, and even how you grow in the future.

Sole Proprietorship

Many entrepreneurs, especially those starting solo, consider the sole proprietorship because it's the simplest structure. I get it—you just want to get started, and the idea of minimal paperwork and immediate control is tempting. But there's a catch: in a sole proprietorship, you and your business are one and the same. That means if your business faces a lawsuit or debt, your personal assets are on the line.

When I was starting out, this was a risk I wasn't willing to take, especially in a field as litigious as the legal field. The same goes for other industries with high-risk factors. However, if your business is low-risk and you're looking to keep things small, this might be a viable option.

But here's the thing—I always advise people to look beyond the short term. If you plan to grow, hire employees, or take on significant projects, the sole proprietorship's lack of liability protection could become a major issue. You'll also have to handle all the profits and losses on your personal tax return, which can complicate your finances as your business grows.

I decided against this option for several reasons. First, dissatisfied customers are almost inevitable in every business. I am sure that even at your favorite restaurant, you have probably had at least one unpleasant experience. It happens. Next, as a homeowner, I didn't want to risk putting my assets on the line.

Limited Liability Company (LLC)

After considering my options, I leaned towards forming an LLC, and it's a choice that many entrepreneurs find appealing. Why? Because an LLC offers the best of both worlds: the simplicity of a sole proprietorship combined with the liability protection of a corporation. As I weighed the risks and rewards, the idea of protecting my personal assets while still maintaining control over my business operations was compelling.

But forming an LLC isn't just about protection—it's also about flexibility. Discuss options regarding how you should be taxed with your accountant, there may be significant financial benefits.

For instance, in my case, choosing to be taxed as a corporation allowed me to reinvest profits into the business more efficiently, which was crucial during the early growth stages. However, it's important to note that setting up an LLC can be more complex and costly than a sole proprietorship, with more stringent regulatory requirements and ongoing filings. However, the setup varies from state to state. In New Jersey, an LLC can be set up online for nominal fees. But, it may be best to consult with a legal professional to ensure all paperwork is correctly filled out and filed appropriately. New Jersey does require LLC owners to file annual reports, among other things. Consult with a specialist to avoid your business getting penalized.

Partnership

If you're not doing it alone, a partnership might be the structure that makes the most sense. Partnerships allow you to share responsibility, resources, and risks with one or more partners. There are different types of partnerships, and understanding these differences is key to making the right choice.

General Partnership (GP): In a GP, all partners share equal responsibility for the business's operations and debts. This was a route I considered when thinking about expanding my practice with other attorneys. But the risk? Each partner's personal assets could be at stake if the business runs into trouble.

Limited Partnership (LP): If you're looking for a way to bring in investors without giving them too much control, an LP might be the answer. The liability of limited partners is restricted to their investment in the business, making it a less risky option for them while still allowing you to maintain control. However note that in most states, non-lawyers cannot be owners of a law firm.

Limited Liability Partnership (LLP): For those in the legal or medical fields, an LLP offers a layer of protection against the actions of other partners. In my field, where malpractice suits are a reality, this structure provides peace of mind by protecting personal assets from the liabilities of other partners.

Choosing the right structure isn't just a legal formality; it's a strategic decision that will impact your business's future. **I strongly recommend consulting with a business attorney and accountant during this process. Their expertise was invaluable to me as I navigated these decisions, helping ensure that my choices aligned with my jursdictions' legal requirements and my personal financial strategy.**

Naming Your Business

When it came time to name my law firm, I realized just how significant this decision was. The name of your business isn't just a label; it's the first impression clients get, and it says a lot about your brand, your values, and your commitment to your work. But beyond branding, there are important legal and ethical considerations that you need to be aware of.

Legal Restrictions and Compliance

In many industries, and especially in the legal field, there are strict regulations governing business names. For example, in law, you can't just add "and Associates" to your firm's name unless you actually have multiple attorneys working for you. If you're a solo practitioner, naming your firm "Smith & Partners" is not only misleading but could also violate ethical guidelines. Many jurisdictions require that the attorney's name be included in the firm name, especially in solo practices. This not only ensures transparency but also builds personal credibility and trust with clients.

Similarly, you can't use words that imply partnership or specialization unless those claims are legitimate and verifiable. When I named my firm, I had to be very careful to choose a name that reflected my practice's reality while complying with all relevant regulations. A name that suggests an affiliation, partnership, or specialization that doesn't exist can harm your reputation and lead to legal troubles down the line.

It's also crucial to avoid using names that could imply a level of expertise or certification that you don't have. For instance, using terms like "experts" or "specialists" in your business name without the appropriate credentials could lead to serious ethical violations and even disciplinary actions. Please review all guidelines set by the American Bar Association and various local state bar associations to ensure compliance. Ethics isn't just a buzzword; it's the backbone of any reputable business. Your business name should never mislead potential clients about the nature of your services.

Strategic Naming for Branding and Growth

Beyond legal and ethical considerations, your business name is a critical part of your brand identity. It needs to be memorable, easy to pronounce, and resonate with your target audience. I spent a lot of time thinking about how my firm's name would look on business cards, letterheads, websites, and other marketing materials. The name needed to convey professionalism, reliability, and the type of legal services I offered. I also did a survey of other law firms and how their firms were named.

One thing I realized was the importance of choosing a name that could grow with my business. A name that's too closely tied to a specific location or practice area can limit your ability to diversify or expand. For example, if you name your business "Newark Family Law," it might not be as effective if you later decide to expand into corporate law or to open offices in other cities. If my firm name had "New Jersey" in it, clients from New York may not consider my services because they would assume that I only worked in New Jersey.

Before finalizing your business name, conduct a thorough search to ensure it isn't already in use by another firm or business. This helps avoid potential trademark infringements and the confusion that could arise from a name that's too similar to another established brand.

The Importance of Consulting with Professionals

Starting a business involves navigating a complex landscape of legal, financial, and regulatory requirements. While you might be an expert in your field, managing the business side of things often requires a different skill set. This is where consulting with professionals—like an accountant and attorney—becomes invaluable. They can provide the expertise you need to set up your business correctly, avoid costly mistakes, and ensure compliance with all relevant laws and regulations.

Working With an Accountant

An accountant (especially a certified public accountant) is crucial to the financial health of your business. When I was starting out, my accountant helped me analyze the tax implications of different business structures, which played a significant role in my decision to form an LLC. They can also help you set up an accounting system for your business, ensuring that your financial records are accurate, organized, and compliant with regulatory standards. This is especially important as your business grows and the complexity of your finances increases. As a self-employed person, you may be required to file quarterly taxes. We lawyers are not known for our math skills, so having a CPA on speed dial could be very handy.

Your accountant can also assist in developing a budget, managing cash flow, bookkeeping, and developing a system for payroll. These are all critical aspects of running a successful business, and having professional guidance can make a world of difference. For me, having an accountant I could trust meant I could focus on building my practice while knowing that the financial side of things was in good hands.

Most solo practitioners that get into trouble are usually cited/censored for issues related to finances. Your license is a privilege, not a right. Invest in setting up proper financial systems to avoid jeopardizing your livelihood due to silly mistakes.

Legal Advice and Risk Management

Consulting with an attorney is equally important, especially when it comes to legal compliance and risk management. An attorney who specializes in helping startups can assist you in drafting and reviewing contracts, such as client engagement agreements, partnership agreements, and leases for office space. These documents are vital for protecting your interests and ensuring your business operations are legally sound.

In my experience, having a legal advisor from the outset helped me navigate the complexities of business law, including understanding the regulatory requirements specific to my industry. They also provided valuable insights into risk management, helping me implement strategies to mitigate potential legal liabilities. This proactive approach to legal compliance and risk management not only protected my business but also gave me peace of mind as I focused on growing my practice. Keep in mind that as a lawyer, this may be as simple as asking for advice from a colleague who is already out on their own. But, you have a duty to do your own research to ensure that your company is complying with all applicable regulations and laws.

Your local bar associations may also have relevant resources so definitely check out their websites.

CHAPTER 2

Market Research and Planning

Starting and growing a successful business, whether it's a law firm or any other type of business, is a journey that requires careful planning and a deep understanding of the market you're entering. The importance of market research and planning cannot be overstated—these steps lay the foundation for everything that follows.

When I decided to start my law firm, I knew that understanding the market and creating a solid business plan would be crucial to my success. I kept track of the types of legal issues people requested assistance with to gauge which practice areas were in high demand.

This chapter will take you through the process of identifying your target clientele, conducting competitive analysis, creating a detailed business plan, and securing the necessary funding to bring your vision to life.

Identifying Your Target Clientele

The first step in building a successful business is identifying who you want to serve. For me, this meant figuring out the type of clients I wanted to represent in my law firm. I knew that my passion lay in helping individuals facing legal challenges, particularly those who were negligently, intentionally, or recklessly injured. I also knew from my time as a law clerk that criminal justice was also an area where people like me were needed, and criminal defense was an area I was passionate about. But beyond that, I had to think about the specific demographics, needs, and preferences of my ideal clients. I also had to consider which practice areas could be lucrative enough to help me sustain my business.

For those who want to get started and are unsure what practice areas they want to specialize in, when you're identifying your target clientele, you need to ask yourself some key questions:

- *Who are they?*

Are they individuals, small business owners, or large corporations? What age group do they belong to? What are their income levels? Where are they located? Understanding the demographics of your target market is crucial. For example, understanding the income level will help you create an appealing billing structure. For many potential clients, flat fees seem less daunting than billing. But if you mostly work with corporations, billing is typically the norm.

- *What are their needs and pain points?*

What specific problems or challenges are they facing that your business can solve? For a law firm, this might be clients who need legal representation in personal injury cases, criminal defense, or workers' compensation matters. For other businesses, it could be customers looking for a particular product or service.

- *What motivates them?*

What drives their decision-making? Is it price, quality, convenience, or something else? Understanding the motivations of your target clientele will help you tailor your services and marketing efforts to meet their needs.

- *Where can you find them?*

What platforms do they use to search for services? Are they active on social media, or do they rely on word-of-mouth referrals? Knowing where to find your target clients is essential for effective marketing.

In my case, I realized early on that many of my potential clients were individuals who were unfamiliar with the legal process and needed someone to guide them through it. They were often scared, confused, and in need of a lawyer who not only had the expertise but also the empathy to understand their situation. This realization shaped the way I marketed my services, how I communicated with clients, and even the way I structured my fee arrangements.

As a new business owner, opportunities to advertise will be everywhere. One must be strategic in how funds are invested, especially early on. You do not want to waste money advertising in places where your target audience will not see it. For example, I was offered a contract to advertise in a gym early on. The price was phenomenal, and they had locations all over.

However, as a personal injury attorney, I had to think about this decision. Ultimately, I decided that most of my target clients would not be going to the gym after accidents. Thus, I decided to forego locking myself into that contract.

In sum, identifying your target clientele isn't a one-time task—it's an ongoing process. As your business grows, you may find that your ideal clientele profile evolves. Maybe you start off serving individuals, but over time, you realize that small business owners or other types of clients are better suited for your services. This is what happened to me.

Originally, I began only doing personal injury. But personal injury and workers' compensation are so related that I ended up also handling workers' compensation. Then, I slowly began building a criminal defense practice, too. The key is to remain flexible and open to refining your target market as you gather more insights and experience.

However, the expansion of my practice areas will likely end there. The worst thing you can do as an attorney is be a jack of all trades and a master of none.

Conducting Competitive Analysis

Once you've identified your target clientele, the next step is understanding the competitive landscape. When I was planning for my law firm, I knew that I wasn't the only lawyer offering personal injury and criminal defense services. There were other firms, some well-established, that I would be competing against. Understanding what these competitors were doing—and where I could differentiate myself—was crucial.

Here's how I approached competitive analysis and how you can, too:

- *Identify Your Competitors*

Start by identifying who your direct competitors are. These are businesses that offer similar services or products to the same target market. For a law firm, this could be other firms in your area specializing in the same practice areas. For other types of businesses, it could be companies that offer a similar product or service.

- *Analyze Their Strengths and Weaknesses*

What are your competitors doing well? Where are they falling short? Look at their marketing strategies, client reviews, pricing, and service offerings. For example, I noticed that some of my competitors had a strong online presence but lacked the personal touch that clients needed during stressful legal situations. This insight helped me position my firm as one that not only had legal expertise but also offered a compassionate, client-centered approach.

▪ *Differentiate Your Business*

Identify ways to differentiate your business from the competition based on your analysis. What unique value can you offer that your competitors don't? For me, it was my commitment to advocacy and my personal experience in the insurance industry that allowed me to better understand and fight for my clients' rights.

It was also my commitment to sustainable growth and avoiding taking on more cases than I could reasonably handle. Maybe for your business, it's a unique product feature, exceptional customer service, or a more competitive pricing model.

▪ *Keep an Eye on Market Trends*

The competitive landscape is always changing, so it's important to stay informed about industry trends, new entrants into the market, and changes in consumer behavior. It is also important to keep up with changes in the law to ensure that your business is compliant. This will help you adapt your strategy and stay ahead of the competition.

Competitive analysis isn't just about knowing who you're up against—it's about using that knowledge to make strategic decisions that will set your business apart. When I started my firm, I wasn't interested in simply copying what others were doing. I wanted to carve out my own niche and offer something unique that would resonate with my target clients. By thoroughly analyzing the competition, I was able to do just that.

Creating a Detailed Business Plan and Financial Projections

A solid business plan is the blueprint for your success. It's a document that outlines your business goals, strategies, and the steps you'll take to achieve them. When I started my law firm, I knew that having a detailed business plan was essential—not just for securing funding but also for keeping me focused and on track.

Your business plan should include the following key components:

- *Executive Summary*

This is a brief overview of your business, including your mission statement, the services or products you offer, and your business goals. Think of it as the elevator pitch for your business. When I wrote my executive summary, I focused on my commitment to advocacy and my unique background in the insurance industry, which gave me a competitive edge in personal injury cases. I also gave some details regarding my specific practice area and what makes it lucrative.

- *Business Description*

Describe the services or products your business will offer. For a law firm, this might include different practice areas, such as personal injury, criminal defense, or family law. For other businesses, it could be a range of products or services tailored to your target market. In my business plan, I highlighted the specific legal services I would offer and how they aligned with the needs of my target clients.

- *Market Analysis*

This section should include the insights you gained from your market research and competitive analysis. Describe your target clientele, the market size, and the trends affecting your industry. For my law firm, I included information about the demand for personal injury and criminal defense services in my area, as well as the competitive landscape. I also included descriptions of the major players and main activities in my practice areas.

- *Organizational/Legal Structure*

Outline the structure of your business, including the roles and responsibilities of key team members. Also, detail the legal structure of your business (i.e. whether it is an LLC, S-Corp, etc). If you're a solo entrepreneur, this section might be simpler, but it's still important to define your own role and any support staff or outsourced services you'll need.

I was a one-person operation when I started, but I still included plans for future growth, such as hiring additional attorneys or administrative staff. I also included allowances for a full-time assistant in all of my projections. This came in handy as, within one week of starting my firm, I had to hire an assistant to help me with the tasks that I did not have time for.

- *SWOT Analysis*

My business plan contained a SWOT analysis. Anyone with a business background knows that SWOT stands for Strengths, Weaknesses, Opportunities, and Threats. This should be a realistic outline for yourself and for any potential lenders. Having a comprehensive analysis allows you to think strategically about your business and any areas of potential weaknesses that you have to strengthen. It also helps you strategize about the ways you can grow.

- *Operational Plan*

This will detail your role in the company and all proposed roles in your startup. This should include hours of operation, the hours the employees will be working (e.g. 40 hours per week, per diem, part-time, etc.), the tasks that the employees will be responsible for, and other details relevant to daily operations.

- *Marketing and Sales Strategy*

Detail your plans for attracting and retaining clients or customers. This should include your branding, marketing channels, and sales tactics. For my firm, I focused on building a strong online presence, leveraging my network for referrals, and providing exceptional client service to generate positive word-of-mouth. I also tried to think outside of the box and find ways to reach potential clients via avenues not already saturated by bigger firms.

■ *Financial Projections*

This section is critical for demonstrating the financial viability of your business. Include detailed projections for revenue, expenses, and profits over the next three to five years. Be realistic but also optimistic—show potential investors or lenders that you have a clear path to profitability.

When I created my financial projections, I factored in my existing client base, expected growth, and the costs associated with running a law firm. It is admittedly difficult to calculate potential profits. I was able to do so by asking several solo practitioners how much they made in their first year and taking an average. I then worked with my CPA to create more accurate projections.

- *Funding Request (if applicable)*

If you're seeking external funding, this section should outline how much money you need, what you'll use it for, and how you plan to repay it. When I started my firm, I was fortunate to have a small client base that followed me, but I still required external funding. I had to ensure I would be able to pay myself and my employees before my business began generating revenue. Most lenders will ask for your projections to be sent separately via Excel.

- *Appendix*

Include any additional information that supports your business plan, such as resumes, legal documents, or detailed financial data. For me, this included my resume, client testimonials, and some preliminary marketing materials I had developed. It also included details regarding my background in business, including getting a degree in economics and my time running other businesses. What most people do not know is that my law firm was the fifth "official" business I started.

I previously did property management, was a landlord, owned a trucking company, sold skincare products, sold digital products, provided resume services, and the list goes on. Detailing all of my experience as a business owner made lenders take me seriously. Regardless of the outcome of your prior businesses, that experience will separate you from your competitors.

A well-thought-out business plan serves as a roadmap for your business, guiding you through the ups and downs of entrepreneurship. It's a living document that you should revisit and update regularly as your business evolves.

When I first started, my business plan was a critical tool that helped me stay focused on my goals and make informed decisions. It also gave me the confidence to approach potential clients and partners, knowing that I had a clear vision for my firm's success.

Securing Funding Through Loans, Grants, or Personal Investment

One of the biggest challenges for any new business is securing the funding needed to get off the ground. When I started my law firm, I had to think carefully about how to manage my finances and ensure I had enough capital to cover my expenses.

With past business ventures, I made the mistake of not doing this. This led to there never being enough funds to pay myself. That was a big mistake, but it was sustainable because I still worked full-time. With my law firm, I went all in, i.e., I quit my full-time job. So, operating like this would have never been sustainable. I had to ensure that I would be able to pay myself and maintain my lifestyle, even if revenue generation had not begun. I had no idea that companies would provide funding for this.

There are several options for funding a new business, and the right choice for you will depend on your specific circumstances:

- *Personal Savings*

Using personal savings is one of the most straightforward ways to fund your business. It involves dipping into your own financial resources to cover startup costs. This approach has several advantages: it doesn't involve taking on debt or giving away equity and shows potential investors or lenders that you're committed to your business. However, I myself and many other entrepreneurs believe in the fundamental philosophy of OPM., i.e., other people's money. It is my personal belief that your personal savings should not be used to start a new business. There are so many grants, loans, and other funding options available. Why put your livelihood on the line when there are billion-dollar corporations willing to fund your dreams?

- *Bank Loans*

Bank loans are a common way to finance a new business. They provide a lump sum of money that you repay with interest over time. To secure a bank loan, you'll need to present a solid business plan, demonstrate your ability to repay the loan, and possibly provide collateral.

When preparing for a bank loan application, make sure your business plan is comprehensive and up-to-date. Lenders will want to see detailed financial projections, a clear plan for how the loan funds will be used, and evidence of your ability to manage and grow the business. I found that having a detailed plan and demonstrating my prior client base helped strengthen my application.

- *Loans via the SBA*

The Small Business Association (SBA) has partnered with several banks to provide startup loans for small businesses. Applications for microloans (loans under $50,000) are a lot less rigorous than applications for larger loans. Consider applying via an approved SBA lender, as it may be simpler for you to obtain financing versus going through a traditional bank.

Do not let interest deter you. If a company gives you $50,000 to start your business and over 5 years you have to pay back let's say, $5,000 (10% interest), this may be worth it. You are essentially paying $1,000 a year to get $50,000 up front to start and build the business of your dreams.

- *Grants*

Business grants are another potential source of funding, though they can be highly competitive and difficult to obtain. Grants are typically provided by government agencies, foundations, or nonprofit organizations and do not require repayment. They are often awarded for specific purposes, such as supporting startups in certain industries or serving underserved communities.

While grants can be an excellent source of funding, they require a significant amount of effort to apply for. You'll need to prepare detailed proposals and demonstrate how your business aligns with the grant's objectives. In my experience, while grants were not a primary funding source, researching and applying for relevant grants can be beneficial, especially if they align with your business goals and values.

You may also want to consider paying someone to apply for grants for you. However, because you still may not win the grant, I would not pay a hefty sum for this service.

- *Angel Investors*

Angel investors are individuals who invest their personal funds in startups in exchange for equity or convertible debt. They often bring more than just money to the table—they can provide valuable advice, mentorship, and connections. Angel investors are typically interested in high-growth potential businesses and might be willing to take on more risk compared to traditional lenders.

When approaching angel investors, it's important to have a clear pitch and a compelling business plan. Investors will want to understand your business model, market opportunity, and how you plan to generate returns on their investment. I know several colleagues who began their businesses using funds secured from angel investors in their personal networks.

■ *Crowdfunding*

Crowdfunding platforms allow you to raise small amounts of money from a large number of people, usually through online platforms. It can be a way to raise funds while also building a community around your business. There are several platforms which allow you to present your business idea to potential backers and offer various incentives for their support.

Crowdfunding can also serve as a marketing tool, creating buzz and validating your business idea. However, it requires a strong marketing campaign and effective communication to attract backers. I found that while crowdfunding was an intriguing option, it wasn't the best fit for my law firm. Still, it's worth considering if you have a product or service that could resonate with a broad audience.

- *Strategic Partnerships*

Partnering with other businesses or professionals can also be a way to secure funding or resources. For example, forming alliances with other service providers or businesses can lead to joint ventures where costs and revenues are shared. These partnerships can provide access to new client bases, shared marketing opportunities, and additional funding sources.

When I started my firm, I considered partnerships with other legal professionals and organizations. While it didn't result in direct funding, it did offer opportunities for collaboration and client referrals, which were valuable as I built my practice.

There are also several opportunities to become a per diem or contract attorney for government entities within your state. This can be a great way to ensure that money is always coming in, especially for practice areas that are based on contingency, i.e., sometimes, you may have to wait years before you are paid for your services.

Securing funding is often one of the most challenging aspects of starting a business, but it's also a crucial step that can determine your ability to succeed. Whether you use personal savings, apply for bank loans, seek grants, attract investors, or explore other funding options, the key is to approach the process with a clear plan and a realistic understanding of your needs and goals. Each funding option comes with its own set of advantages and challenges, so it's important to choose the one that aligns best with your business model and long-term vision. It is also important to ensure your projections are realistic so you can avoid running into cash flow problems.

When I was building my firm, the combination of an SBA loan, client retention, and strategic planning helped me navigate the financial aspects of starting a business. Your journey might look different, but with careful planning and strategic use of resources, you can set your business up for success.

PART II: SETTING UP

YOUR PRACTICE

CHAPTER 3

Essential Tools and Technology

"The best preparation for tomorrow is doing your best today."

— *H. Jackson Brown Jr.*

When it comes to setting up a successful practice, whether you're a solo attorney or running a growing firm, choosing the right tools and technology is crucial. This chapter will delve into the essential software and hardware considerations that can make or break your efficiency and productivity.

Drawing from my own experiences and insights, I'll guide you through selecting case management software and research tools and setting up your office with the right equipment. The aim is not just to get you started but to ensure you're equipped with the best resources to manage your practice effectively and sustainably.

Selecting Case Management Software

When I first started my practice, I never underestimated the sheer volume of paperwork that case management required. On day one, it was clear that having an efficient system was not just a convenience but a necessity. Case management software is the backbone of your practice's operations. It's where you'll track case progress, manage deadlines, communicate with clients, and store crucial documents.

Assessing Your Needs

Before diving into the sea of available software options, start by evaluating your needs. Are you a solo practitioner or part of a larger team? Do you specialize in a particular area of law that requires unique features? For instance, if you handle a high volume of personal injury cases, you'll need software that can manage a lot of client information, track medical records, and handle settlements.

You may also want a system that can generate reports so that you can track upcoming statutes. If you're in criminal defense, you might need robust tools for case notes and courtroom schedules.

The best way to get acquainted with software is to request trials from the different service providers. I had several meetings with different providers and tracked the features provided by each of them. I wanted a provider that could track emails related to each case, run reports, allow me to keep case notes, allow me to store insurance information, and which could automate documents that we frequently use. I wanted a software that could seamlessly integrate with my email software, calendar, and document management systems.

Cost Considerations

Case management software can range from affordable to quite expensive. Consider your budget, but also weigh the potential return on investment. The right software can save you time and reduce errors, ultimately increasing your profitability. Many providers offer free trials, so take advantage of these to test the software before committing. Also, consider the cost to add new users as your firm grows.

Implementation Tips

Once you've selected your software, invest time in training yourself and your staff. Effective implementation can significantly impact your productivity. Develop standard operating procedures for using the software to ensure consistency across your practice.

Research Software and Databases

Research is at the heart of legal practice. Whether you're drafting a brief, preparing for a case, or seeking precedents, having reliable research tools is essential. In my journey, I've come to rely on several key databases and research software that have proven invaluable.

Choosing the Right Research Tools

Here are some considerations and recommendations based on my experience:

- Westlaw: One of the leading legal research tools, Westlaw offers comprehensive databases of case law, statutes, and secondary sources. Its advanced search capabilities and extensive resources make it a go-to for in-depth legal research.

- LexisNexis: Similar to Westlaw, LexisNexis provides a vast array of legal information and research tools. It also offers analytical tools and practice-specific content that can be incredibly useful depending on your area of practice.

- Fastcase: Fastcase is known for its cost-effectiveness and robust search functionality. It's a good alternative for firms looking to keep research costs down without sacrificing quality.

Utilizing Research Tools Effectively

To maximize the benefits of your research tools:

- Stay Updated: Legal databases are constantly updated with new case law and statutes. Regularly check for updates to ensure you're using the most current information.

- Leverage Advanced Features: Many research tools offer advanced features like citation analysis and legal research aids. Take the time to learn and use these features to enhance your research efficiency.

- Organize Your Findings: Use the research tool features to organize and categorize your findings. This will make it easier to retrieve relevant information quickly when needed.

Balancing Cost and Benefit

Research tools can be expensive, but the cost is often justified by the value they provide. Consider your practice's needs and budget when choosing a tool. Many firms use a combination of free and paid resources to balance cost and functionality.

Office Setup and Equipment

Your office setup plays a significant role in your daily operations. A well-organized, functional workspace can enhance productivity and create a professional environment for your clients. Here's what I've learned about setting up an effective office:

Essential Equipment

- Computers and Peripherals: Invest in high-quality computers with sufficient processing power to handle your case management and research software. Don't forget essential peripherals like printers, scanners, and reliable backup drives.

- Office Furniture: Choose ergonomic furniture that supports long hours of work. A comfortable chair and a functional desk can make a big difference in your productivity and health. A couch is fantastic for litigators like myself. I love lounging on my couch for a quick 20-minute break after lengthy court sessions.

- Communication Tools: Reliable phones and conferencing equipment are crucial, especially if you're handling remote consultations or court appearances. Consider investing in a good-quality headset for clear communication during calls and virtual meetings.

Technology Integration

Ensure that your office equipment integrates well with your software systems. For example, if you're using cloud-based case management software, ensure that your computers and other devices are compatible and secure. This integration can streamline your workflow and reduce technical issues. You may want to hire a small, local technology company to assist with this.

Additionally, you may want to consider investing in a work phone. When I first began, I had all my work calls coming to my cell phone. This quickly became very overwhelming. Investing in a work cell phone allows me to have a better work-life balance. It allows me to put away my work cell when I am having family time and to put away my personal cell when I am at work.

Security Considerations

Security is a top priority in any legal practice. Invest in robust cybersecurity measures, including antivirus software, firewalls, and secure data storage solutions. Regularly update your security protocols to protect sensitive client information from potential threats.

Creating a Productive Work Environment

Your office setup should facilitate productivity. Organize your workspace to minimize distractions and keep essential documents and tools within easy reach. A clean and orderly environment can improve your focus and efficiency.

Adapting to Remote Work

With the rise of remote work, consider setting up a home office if necessary. Ensure that your home office is equipped with the same technology and security measures as your main office. Adapt your workflows to include remote communication and document-sharing tools to stay connected with clients and colleagues.

There are firms that are completely remote and only rent conference rooms when necessary. This may be a great cost saver, as office rent can be expensive and unnecessary depending on the type of business. Especially in the beginning when you may not have a large clientele. There are also tax benefits because a portion of your mortgage/rent can be written off as a business expense. Consult with a CPA for details.

Investing in the right tools and technology is a crucial step in setting up your practice. From case management software to office equipment, the choices you make will impact your efficiency and effectiveness. By carefully selecting and implementing these resources, you'll set yourself up for success in managing your practice and serving your clients effectively.

CHAPTER 4

Building Your Team

"If you want to go fast, go alone. If you want to go far, go together."

— *African Proverb*

As your practice grows, the demands on your time and energy will inevitably increase. While starting as a solo practitioner may seem manageable at first, there comes a point where trying to do it all yourself becomes counterproductive. The key to scaling your practice and maintaining a high standard of service is building the right team. In this chapter, I'll guide you through the essentials of staffing for a solo practitioner, including when to hire, what roles to consider, and how to effectively manage virtual assistants or employees.

Staffing Needs for a Solo Practitioner

As a solo practitioner, you might start your journey by handling every aspect of your practice on your own. From answering phones and managing appointments to drafting legal documents and meeting with clients, you're likely wearing many hats. This all-in-one approach works well in the beginning, especially when your caseload is manageable. However, as your practice grows, so do the demands on your time and energy. You'll reach a point where juggling all these responsibilities becomes overwhelming, and the quality of your work might begin to suffer. That's when you'll realize that building a team is not just an option— it's a necessity.

Identifying the Right Time to Hire

Recognizing the right time to bring in help is crucial to maintaining the quality of your practice while allowing it to grow. One of the first signs that it's time to hire is when your workload consistently exceeds what you can handle within a standard workday.

If you find yourself working late into the night, sacrificing weekends, and still feeling like you're barely keeping up, it's time to consider bringing someone on board. Not only will this alleviate your stress, but it will also ensure that your clients continue to receive the attention they deserve.

Another clear indicator that it's time to hire is when you're spending a significant amount of time on tasks that are outside your area of expertise. For example, if you're a lawyer who's spending hours each week managing your books, handling marketing, or dealing with IT issues, it's a sign that these tasks should be delegated.

Your primary focus should be on practicing law, and delegating non-legal tasks to someone more skilled in those areas will improve efficiency and allow you to dedicate more time to billable work.

Finally, if you notice a decline in the quality of service you're able to provide, or if clients are experiencing delays because you're spread too thin, it's time to consider hiring. Your reputation is one of the most valuable assets in your practice, and maintaining high standards is critical. By bringing in additional help, you can ensure that each client receives the attention and service they deserve, which will help you maintain a positive reputation and attract more business in the long run.

Deciding What Roles to Fill First

Once you've determined that it's time to hire, the next step is deciding which roles to fill first. For many solo practitioners, the first hire is typically an administrative assistant or a paralegal. These roles are essential because they handle the non-billable and time-consuming tasks that often prevent you from focusing on your core legal work.

An administrative assistant is an excellent first hire because they can take over the day-to-day administrative duties that eat up your time. This includes answering phones, scheduling appointments, managing emails, and handling client intake. By delegating these tasks to an administrative assistant, you free up your time to focus on the aspects of your practice that directly generate revenue, such as client consultations and court appearances.

A paralegal is another valuable addition to your team, particularly if you handle a high volume of cases. Paralegals can assist with substantive legal work, such as drafting documents, conducting legal research, and preparing for trials. Their support can significantly increase your efficiency, allowing you to take on more clients without compromising on the quality of your work. Additionally, paralegals can help you maintain a consistent workflow, ensuring that all necessary tasks are completed in a timely manner.

As you consider which roles to fill first, it's essential to think about how each hire will contribute to the growth and efficiency of your practice. Every team member should bring value to your practice, either by freeing up your time to focus on billable work or by enhancing the services you offer to your clients. This strategic approach to hiring will help you build a team that supports your practice's growth while maintaining high standards of service.

Balancing Costs with Benefits

Hiring additional staff is a significant investment, so it's essential to balance the costs with the benefits. Salaries, benefits, and other associated costs can add up quickly, and as a solo practitioner, you may be concerned about the financial impact. However, it's important to view hiring as an investment in the growth and success of your practice.

Consider the potential return on investment (ROI) when making hiring decisions. For example, if hiring an administrative assistant allows you to take on additional clients, the revenue generated from those clients can offset the cost of the assistant's salary. Similarly, if a paralegal helps you handle more cases efficiently, the increased billable hours can significantly boost your income. The key is to ensure that each hire contributes to the overall profitability of your practice.

To manage costs effectively, you might consider starting with part-time or contract employees before transitioning to full-time staff. This approach allows you to gauge the impact of the additional help on your practice without committing to a full-time salary. As your practice continues to grow and the demand for additional support increases, you can then consider transitioning these roles to full-time positions.

Planning for Future Growth

When building your team, it's important to think about the future. As your practice grows, your staffing needs will likely evolve. You might start with an administrative assistant and a paralegal, but as your client base expands, you may find the need to hire additional support staff or even another attorney.

Planning for future growth means being strategic about your hiring decisions. Consider how each new hire fits into your long-term vision for your practice. Are you planning to expand into new areas of law? Do you want to increase your caseload? Will you need additional support as your client base grows? By thinking ahead and planning for these eventualities, you can build a team that not only meets your current needs but also supports the future growth of your practice.

This will also help you properly budget. Not all "revenue" should be treated as disposable income. You will need to save for future expenses.

Hiring and Managing Virtual Assistants or Employees

In today's digital age, the concept of a traditional office with all employees working in the same physical space is becoming increasingly outdated in some industries. For solo practitioners, hiring virtual assistants (VAs) or remote employees offers a flexible, cost-effective solution to staffing needs.

Virtual assistants can handle a wide range of tasks, from administrative work to specialized legal research, without the need for physical office space or the overhead costs associated with traditional employees. However, successfully hiring and managing VAs or remote employees requires careful planning and a clear understanding of how to integrate them into your practice.

Understanding the Benefits of Virtual Assistants

Virtual assistants offer numerous benefits for solo practitioners, particularly those who are looking to scale their practice without the commitment of hiring full-time, in-office staff. One of the most significant advantages is cost savings. Because VAs work remotely, you save on overhead costs, such as office space, utilities, and equipment. Additionally, many virtual assistants work on a contract basis, which means you're not responsible for providing benefits, like health insurance or paid time off.

Another advantage of virtual assistants is flexibility. You can hire a VA on an as-needed basis, whether that's for a few hours a week or full-time support during particularly busy periods. This flexibility allows you to scale your support based on your current workload without committing to a full-time employee. Virtual assistants can also provide specialized skills that you might not need full-time, such as graphic design, social media management, or advanced legal research.

Furthermore, virtual assistants can help you maintain a better work-life balance. By delegating routine tasks to a VA, you can free up time to focus on higher-level work, spend more time with your family, or simply enjoy some downtime. This can be particularly beneficial for solo practitioners, who often find themselves working long hours to keep up with the demands of their practice.

When I first began, I answered all calls. Not only did this become overwhelming and cumbersome, as my client base grew, it also became infeasible. Delegating this task to a VA has helped free up time and also eliminated the need for my involvement with mundane calls.

Identifying Tasks to Delegate

Once you've decided to hire a virtual assistant, the next step is to identify which tasks you can delegate. The key to successful delegation is to focus on tasks that are important but not necessarily the best use of your time. These are often repetitive, administrative tasks that can be easily handled by someone else, allowing you to concentrate on more complex and billable work.

Common tasks that can be delegated to a VA include managing your calendar, scheduling appointments, answering emails, and handling client communications. A VA can also take over administrative duties, such as invoicing, bookkeeping, and managing your practice's social media accounts. If you handle a large volume of documents, a VA can assist with document preparation, formatting, and filing.

For solo practitioners who need more specialized support, virtual assistants with legal training can assist with legal research, drafting legal documents, and managing case files. This can be particularly valuable for solo practitioners who handle a high volume of cases or need additional support for complex legal matters. By delegating these tasks to a VA, you can ensure that your practice runs smoothly and efficiently, even during busy periods.

When deciding which tasks to delegate, it's important to consider the skills and experience of the VA you're hiring. Some tasks may require specific legal knowledge or familiarity with certain software tools, so be sure to match the tasks you're delegating with the strengths of your VA.

Finding the Right Virtual Assistant

Finding the right virtual assistant requires a clear understanding of your needs and the skills you're looking for. There are many platforms where you can find VAs, including freelance websites, VA agencies, and professional networks. Each option has its pros and cons, so it's important to choose the one that best fits your needs.

Freelance websites like Upwork, Fiverr, and Freelancer offer a wide range of VAs with varying skills and experience levels. These platforms allow you to post a job listing, review applications, and choose the candidate that best meets your requirements. One advantage of using a freelance platform is the ability to hire VAs on a project-by-project basis, which can be ideal if you have short-term needs or want to test out a VA before committing to a long-term contract.

VA agencies, on the other hand, provide pre-vetted assistants who are often more experienced and specialized. These agencies typically handle the hiring process for you, matching you with a VA who has the skills and experience you need. This can save you time and ensure that you're getting a high-quality assistant, but it may come at a higher cost compared to hiring directly through a freelance platform.

When hiring a virtual assistant, it's important to conduct a thorough interview process to ensure they're a good fit for your practice. Ask about their experience, particularly in the legal field if that's relevant to the tasks you're delegating. You should also ask for references or work samples to verify their skills and reliability. Additionally, discuss their availability and communication preferences to ensure they can meet your needs and work effectively within your practice's schedule.

Managing Remote Employees Effectively

Effective management is key to ensuring a productive working relationship once you've hired a virtual assistant or remote employee. One of the biggest challenges of managing remote workers is maintaining clear communication, as you won't have the benefit of face-to-face interactions. However, with the right tools and strategies, you can overcome this challenge and create a seamless workflow.

First, establish clear communication channels from the outset. Tools like Slack, Microsoft Teams, or Zoom can facilitate real-time communication, while email and case management software can help keep track of tasks and deadlines. It's also important to set regular check-ins, whether that's through weekly meetings, daily updates, or as-needed calls. Regular communication helps keep everyone on the same page and allows you to promptly address any issues or concerns.

Second, set clear expectations for your VA or remote employee. This includes outlining their specific responsibilities, deadlines, and performance metrics. Make sure they understand your practice's goals and how their work contributes to achieving them. Providing detailed instructions and guidelines for each task can help ensure that work is completed to your standards. Additionally, consider creating a shared calendar where deadlines and important dates are visible to everyone involved.

You can also require that they keep a daily task list to ensure that no tasks are missed.

Third, trust your virtual assistant or remote employee to do their job. Micromanaging can undermine their productivity and create unnecessary stress. Instead, focus on providing the resources and support they need to succeed, and then step back and let them take ownership of their work. If you've hired the right person, they'll be capable of handling their tasks without constant supervision.

If not, unfortunately, you may have to terminate them and find another option. It can take a few tries before you find the right fit.

Maintaining a Strong Working Relationship

Maintaining a strong working relationship with your VA or remote employee is essential for long-term success. This begins with mutual respect and open communication. Treat your VA as an integral part of your team, and show appreciation for their contributions. Regularly check in to provide feedback, acknowledge their accomplishments, and discuss any areas for improvement.

Another important aspect of maintaining a strong working relationship is flexibility. Understand that remote workers may have different schedules or time zones, and be willing to accommodate these differences when possible. This flexibility can lead to a more productive and positive working relationship, as your VA will feel supported and valued.

Finally, consider the long-term potential of your relationship with your VA. If they're providing excellent work and are a good fit for your practice, think about ways to grow the relationship over time. This might include increasing their responsibilities, offering additional training, or even transitioning them into a full-time role as your practice continues to grow.

CHAPTER 5

Marketing and Client Acquisition

- *"Marketing is no longer about the stuff that you make, but about the stories you tell." — Seth Godin*

In any business, whether it's a solo law practice or a growing firm, marketing plays a pivotal role in attracting and retaining clients. It's not enough to provide a valuable service; you must also effectively communicate that value to potential clients.

Developing a Strong Online Presence (Website, Social Media)

In the digital age, your online presence is often the first impression prospective clients get of your business. Whether you're a solo practitioner or run a multi-service business, your website and social media profiles serve as digital storefronts. For many businesses, clients may never set foot in your

physical office, but they will explore your digital footprint. So, ensuring that your online presence is professional, inviting, and engaging is essential.

Your Website: The Digital Office

Your website is the foundation of your online presence. It is the most important marketing asset for your business because it's where prospective clients will go to learn more about you and your services. A well-designed website should be user-friendly, visually appealing, and optimized for search engines (SEO). But beyond that, it must communicate your value proposition clearly.

Here are key elements your website should include:

- A Professional Look: A clean, modern design immediately gives clients the impression that you are professional and serious about your business. This also means making sure your website is mobile-friendly, as many users will access it from their phones.

- Clear Branding: Your logo, business name, and tagline should be prominently displayed. Branding creates trust and helps prospective clients remember your firm.

- Services or Product Offerings: Clearly list the services or products your business offers with easy navigation. Each service should have its own page explaining what it includes and how it can benefit the client. In the case of law firms, this could include areas of practice, such as family law, personal injury, or criminal defense.

- About Page: People want to know who they're working with. Include a detailed biography explaining your experience, qualifications, and personal story. This is also the place where you can outline your business values.

- Client Testimonials and Case Studies: Potential clients want to see proof of success.

Including testimonials or short case studies of satisfied clients builds credibility and trust.

- **Contact Information and Call-to-Action:** Make it easy for prospective clients to contact you. A contact form, email, phone number, and physical address (if applicable) should be accessible from every page of your website.

SEO Optimization

Building a beautiful website is only the first step. Without the proper search engine optimization (SEO) strategies, clients may never find it. SEO helps your website rank higher in search engine results for relevant keywords.

To optimize your website:

- **Research Keywords:** Identify and target the most relevant keywords for your business. If you're a personal injury lawyer, for example, "personal injury lawyer in [your city]" should be a priority.

- On-Page SEO: Use these keywords strategically throughout your website—in headers, meta descriptions, and within the body content.

- Blogging: Regularly publishing articles on topics related to your industry will help drive traffic to your site. Not only does this provide value to readers, but it also improves your SEO. For example, if you're a business consultant, blog posts like "5 Tips for Scaling Your Business" can help engage potential clients.

- Link Building: Collaborate with other websites and bloggers to create backlinks to your site. The more authoritative websites linked to your content, the better it will perform in search results.

Social Media: Building Relationships at Scale

Beyond a website, social media platforms are a powerful way to promote your business, build brand recognition, and establish relationships with potential clients. Each platform offers unique ways to connect with your audience.

- Facebook: Great for creating a community around your business. You can post updates, client success stories, and promotions and engage with clients through comments and messages. Facebook ads can also target specific demographics.

- LinkedIn: Particularly important for B2B businesses and professionals. A strong LinkedIn presence can help you establish yourself as a thought leader in your industry by posting articles, engaging in industry groups, and networking with potential clients or collaborators.

- Instagram: If your business involves products or services that lend themselves to visual representation (e.g., graphic design, event planning), Instagram is invaluable for showcasing your work. Behind-the-scenes content, client transformations, or success stories can be displayed in a visually appealing way.

- Twitter: Ideal for quick updates, sharing news, or engaging with trends related to your industry. This platform is useful for staying relevant and up-to-date with current discussions in your field.

Consistency is key when it comes to social media. Posting regularly, interacting with followers, and using hashtags related to your industry will help boost your visibility. Social media marketing is not about constantly promoting your business but rather about building relationships, educating your audience, and offering value.

Traditional Marketing Strategies (Local Directories, Referrals)

While digital marketing is essential, traditional marketing strategies remain effective in many industries. Not all clients will discover your business online; some will come from referrals or more traditional methods.

Local Directories and Listings

In addition to your online efforts, listing your business in local directories remains an effective way to attract clients. For example, Google My Business allows you to appear in local search results, and it's free. Being listed on Google and other local directories helps prospective clients find your business when searching for services in your area.

Here are some additional directories to consider:

- Yelp: Not only restaurants but many service providers benefit from Yelp listings. Customer reviews and rankings help build credibility.

- Chamber of Commerce Listings: Joining your local chamber of commerce is an excellent way to meet other local business owners and get referrals.

- Industry-Specific Directories: For law firms, websites like Avvo or Justia can be useful to enhance your online presence.

Networking and Referrals

One of the most powerful traditional marketing strategies is building a referral network. Word of mouth remains a key driver of business for service providers. The trust built through referrals cannot be underestimated.

Building a referral network takes time, but here's how you can start:

- Build Relationships with Complementary Businesses: If you're a law firm, build relationships with financial advisors or accountants who can refer clients to you. If you're in event planning, network with local venues, caterers, and photographers.

- Offer Incentives: In some cases, offering a small referral fee or incentive to clients or other businesses can encourage them to send clients your way. Please double-check the rules in your state. In New Jersey, referral fees can only be paid by certified attorneys. Additionally, certified attorneys can only pay referral fees to other licensed attorneys.

- Provide Excellent Service: The easiest way to ensure you get referrals is to provide exceptional service that encourages your clients to recommend you to others.

Networking Events and Speaking Engagements

Traditional networking events and speaking engagements are excellent opportunities to present your expertise and meet potential clients. These can include local business meetups, conferences, or even community events. By positioning yourself as a leader in your field, you build trust and brand recognition.

Effective Client Communication and Relationship Building

Once you've acquired clients, retaining them and building strong relationships is essential for long-term success. Client retention is often more valuable than client acquisition because repeat business saves marketing costs and builds stability.

Client Communication

Effective communication is at the heart of any successful client relationship. Whether it's through email, phone, or face-to-face meetings, maintaining clear and transparent communication sets the foundation for trust.

Here's how to ensure effective client communication:

- Regular Updates: Keep your clients informed about the progress of their cases, projects, or work. Even if there's no major development, a brief update assures them that their needs are being met.

- Clarity and Transparency: Be upfront about fees, timelines, and any potential challenges. Honesty builds trust, and clients are more likely to stay loyal if they feel they can rely on you.

- Personalization: Treat each client as an individual. Taking the time to understand their needs and goals, and tailoring your communication accordingly, makes clients feel valued.

Building Relationships for Long-Term Success

Building a strong relationship doesn't end with clear communication; it also involves going the extra mile to make clients feel appreciated.

Here are ways to cultivate these relationships:

- Post-Project Follow-Up: After completing a project or service, follow up with your clients to ensure they're satisfied with the results. This shows your commitment to their success.

- Loyalty Programs: Depending on your business, offering loyalty programs or discounts for repeat customers can encourage clients to return and recommend you to others.

- Request Feedback: Always ask for feedback. Not only does this help you improve, but it also shows clients that their opinions are valued.

Marketing and client acquisition are two critical pillars of any successful business. A robust online presence combined with traditional marketing strategies allows you to reach a broad range of potential clients. Once clients are acquired, effective communication and relationship-building are key to ensuring their satisfaction and long-term loyalty.

PART III: FINANCIAL

MANAGEMENT AND

GROWTH

CHAPTER 6

Fee Structure and Billing

- *"Pricing is the art of capturing value. It is not just about covering costs but about communicating the worth of your services."*

Establishing a well-defined fee structure is one of the most important steps to ensure your business's long-term success. Whether you're operating as a solo entrepreneur, running a small law firm, or growing another service-based enterprise, your ability to price your services appropriately, bill clients effectively, and manage your time will directly impact your profitability.

Determining Your Hourly Rate or Flat Fees

Choosing the right fee structure is essential for maintaining profitability while ensuring that clients perceive your services as valuable. There are two primary models for setting fees: hourly rates and flat fees. The choice between these two depends on the nature of your business, the expectations of your clients, and the specific services you offer.

Hourly Rate

Many service-based businesses, especially law firms and consultants, operate using hourly billing. An hourly rate simply reflects the value of your time. But how do you determine what that time is worth? Setting your hourly rate should take into account several factors.

First, assess your operating costs. This includes everything from office rent, utilities, technology, and equipment to employee salaries, insurance, and even taxes. Additionally, knowing your fixed costs is crucial because your hourly rate must at least cover these costs for your business to be profitable.

Next, you must consider your experience and expertise. If you are an established expert in your field, you can charge a higher hourly rate compared to someone just starting. For example, an experienced attorney specializing in a niche area of law, such as intellectual property or corporate law, can command a premium rate because of the specialized knowledge required.

Another important consideration is market demand. Research the going rates for your industry within your geographical area or market niche. Benchmarking your fees against competitors gives you a realistic idea of what clients are willing to pay and ensures you are not pricing yourself out of the market.

Also, factor in the value to the client. Hourly rates should not just reflect the time spent on a task but also the value your expertise brings. For instance, solving a complex legal issue in a few hours could save your client thousands of dollars, meaning your time is more valuable than the hours you put in.

Once you've factored in these elements, test your rate. Many businesses make the mistake of underpricing themselves, particularly when they are new. Resist this temptation, as it may lead to burnout and devalue your service over time.

As a newer lawyer, it is understandable that you may not want to set your rates too high until you become more experienced. However, as your time grows scarce, you may eventually have no choice.

Flat Fees

For certain types of services, flat fees (or fixed fees) can be a more attractive option for both you and your clients. Flat fees involve charging a set amount for a specific service or package of services, regardless of the time it takes to complete the work.

One of the main advantages of flat fees is predictability. Clients appreciate knowing upfront what they will pay for your services, reducing the fear of unpredictable costs. For businesses, flat fees provide a more consistent cash flow, as you can estimate revenue more accurately based on the number of clients you serve.

To determine your flat fees, you must first break down your services into clearly defined tasks. For example, if you're a lawyer, you could offer flat fees for services like drafting a contract, filing for a trademark, or handling a simple divorce case. If you're a consultant, flat fees might be offered for an initial strategy session or a full audit of a company's operations.

To calculate the fee, consider how long each task typically takes and the value it provides to the client. Flat fees should cover both direct costs (time, materials) and indirect costs (research, consultation, follow-up). However, it's crucial to manage expectations and clearly define what is and is not included in the flat fee to avoid scope creep—when a project expands beyond its initial agreement without additional compensation.

One effective practice is to include something in the retainer that specifies the scope of representation. The retainer agreement can dictate that additional fees will be imposed if the representation goes beyond the anticipated scope. For example, most criminal retainers provide a flat rate but specify that if the case goes to trial, an additional specified rate will be imposed.

Effective Billing and Collection Practices

Your pricing strategy won't matter if you don't have effective systems in place for billing clients and collecting payments. Poor billing practices can lead to cash flow problems and strained client relationships. Implementing efficient billing processes ensures you're paid on time and maintains healthy, long-term relationships with your clients.

Clear and Transparent Invoices

One of the most common frustrations clients face is receiving invoices they don't understand. To avoid disputes and delays in payment, your invoices should be clear, itemized, and transparent. If you're charging by the hour, provide a breakdown of the tasks completed and the hours worked. If you're billing a flat fee, list the services included in that fee. A well-designed invoice should include:

- **Service Description:** Clearly state the service provided, whether it's consultation hours, legal work, or project deliverables.

- **Timeframe:** Include the dates when the work was performed.

- **Payment terms:** Clearly outline when payment is due (e.g., within 30 days of receipt) and whether late fees apply.

- **Payment methods:** Offer multiple ways for clients to pay (bank transfers, credit cards, online payment portals), making it as convenient as possible.

- **Scope of representation:** As stated above, retainer agreements should specify the scope of representation. You may want to ask local attorneys for samples in order to tailor your agreement to the requirements in your jurisdiction.

Automating your billing with invoicing software like QuickBooks, FreshBooks, or Xero can also make the process more seamless. These systems not only create professional-looking invoices but also track payments and send automatic reminders to clients with overdue balances.

Upfront Payments and Retainers

A useful strategy for ensuring prompt payment is to require upfront payments or retainers, especially for large projects or ongoing services. This way, you're protected from doing extensive work without being compensated.

In the legal profession, retainers are common practice, where clients pay a sum upfront, the money is deposited in the firm escrow account, and you deduct from it as you perform services. Other service businesses can adopt a similar approach, requiring a percentage of the total fee before work begins. This provides a financial cushion and reduces the likelihood of late payments.

Managing Late Payments

Despite your best efforts, some clients will inevitably pay late. Having a process in place for dealing with late payments is crucial to maintaining a steady cash flow. The key is to address the issue early before it becomes a major problem.

- **Set Clear Terms:** Always include a payment due date on your invoices. If payment is not received by that date, follow up with a polite reminder within a week.

- **Late Fees:** To encourage timely payment, consider including a clause in your contracts that charges a small late fee after a grace period. This should be communicated to clients upfront so they are aware of the consequences of late payment.

- **Payment Plans:** For clients who are genuinely struggling to pay on time, offering a payment plan can be a win-win solution. This allows them to pay in installments while you still receive your money without having to pursue more aggressive collection tactics.

- **Collection Agencies:** As a last resort, you may need to engage a collection agency to recover unpaid debts. However, this step should be avoided if possible, as it can harm client relationships and involve additional costs.

Time Management and Productivity Tips

Effective fee structure and billing practices are only part of the equation for growing a successful business. Time management is equally important because, as the old adage goes, time is money. The more efficiently you use your time, the more value you can deliver to your clients—and the more revenue you can generate.

Tracking Your Time

To maximize productivity, start by tracking how you spend your time.This data is invaluable, not only for ensuring accurate billing but also for identifying areas where time is being wasted or where you could delegate tasks to others.

Prioritizing Tasks with Time-Blocking

Time-blocking is a powerful time management technique that involves dividing your day into blocks of time and dedicating each block to a specific task or type of work. This ensures you're focused and prevents multitasking, which can lead to distractions and inefficiency.

For example, you might reserve mornings for deep work (e.g., drafting legal documents or consulting with clients) and afternoons for administrative tasks (e.g., billing, emails, client follow-ups). By creating a structured schedule, you can avoid spending too much time on low-value activities and maximize your billable hours.

Delegation and Outsourcing

As your business grows, you'll need to delegate certain tasks to employees or outsource them to freelancers. One of the biggest obstacles to scaling is trying to do everything yourself, as it can lead to burnout and inefficiencies. Delegate administrative tasks (like bookkeeping, scheduling, or marketing) to assistants or agencies so you can focus on high-value work that drives revenue.

Avoiding Overwork and Burnout

While maximizing your billable hours is important, it's equally essential to avoid overworking yourself. Burnout not only affects your health but can also impact the quality of your work and client satisfaction. Set boundaries around your working hours and schedule regular breaks to recharge. This will allow you to be more productive and maintain a higher level of performance over the long term.

Establishing the right fee structure and billing practices, while optimizing your time management, is fundamental to running a successful business. Whether you're determining your hourly rate or adopting flat fees, clear and transparent billing and strong client communication are essential.

Coupled with effective time management techniques, these strategies will enable you to maximize profitability, ensure timely payments, and maintain long-lasting client relationships.

Understanding Escrow Accounts for Attorneys

In the legal profession, managing client funds with integrity is paramount. One of the critical tools that attorneys use to ensure the proper handling of client funds is the escrow account. Before you hang your shingle, ensure you understand how accounting for law firms works. Even though you should definitely consult with a certified public accountant, you must also have an understanding of how your accounting system works. Most solo-practitioners get into trouble for issues involving finances.

What is an Escrow Account?

An escrow account is a financial arrangement where a third party temporarily holds funds on behalf of two parties involved in a transaction. In the legal context, attorneys often use escrow accounts to manage client funds, such as retainers, settlement funds, or any money that must be held in trust for clients. The key purpose of an escrow account is to provide security and ensure that the funds are only released when specific conditions are met.

Why Attorneys Need Escrow Accounts

For many attorneys, especially those dealing with real estate, family law, or personal injury cases, escrow accounts are a legal requirement. They provide a safeguard for client funds and help maintain transparency in financial transactions. Mismanagement of client funds can lead to severe legal repercussions, including disciplinary action from state bar associations. Thus, it is crucial for attorneys to understand the rules governing escrow accounts in their jurisdiction.

A $100 mistake seems small, but it could cost you your license.

Types of Funds Held in Escrow Accounts

Attorneys may hold various types of funds in escrow accounts, including:

- Retainers: Initial fees paid by clients to secure legal services.

- Settlement Funds: Money from a settlement agreement that needs to be distributed among clients or third parties.

- Trust Funds: Funds held for clients until they are disbursed for specific purposes, such as paying bills or settling debts.

Legal Requirements for Escrow Accounts

Each jurisdiction has specific rules governing escrow accounts, including how funds should be held, recorded, and disbursed. It is vital for attorneys to familiarize themselves with these regulations to avoid potential pitfalls. Many state bar associations require attorneys to undergo specific training or continuing education courses related to escrow account management.

How to Set Up an Escrow Account

Setting up an escrow account involves several steps:

- **Choose a Financial Institution:** Select a bank or credit union that offers escrow account services and meets any specific requirements set by your state bar association.

- **Open the Account:** Open the escrow account under your law firm's name and ensure it is distinct from your personal and operational accounts.

- **Document Everything:** Keep meticulous records of all transactions involving the escrow account, including deposits, withdrawals, and the purpose of each transaction.

- **Regular Reconciliation:** Regularly reconcile your escrow account with your financial institution to ensure that your records match the bank statements. This practice helps identify any discrepancies early and maintains transparency.

Managing Funds in Escrow Accounts

Properly managing an escrow account involves several best practices:

- **Separate Client Funds:** Always keep client funds in separate escrow accounts, distinct from your firm's operating funds. This separation protects both you and your clients.

- **Maintain Transparency:** Be transparent with clients about how their funds are being managed. Regular updates on the status of their funds can foster trust and strengthen your client relationship.

- **Disbursement Procedures:** Establish clear procedures for disbursing funds from the escrow account. Ensure that funds are only released when all conditions have been met and documented.

- **Register your account: New Jersey requires that attorney escrow accounts**

be registered. Be sure to check to see what your local jurisdiction requires.

Accounting for Escrow Accounts

Accounting for escrow accounts requires diligent record-keeping. Here are some steps to ensure proper accounting:

- **Track All Transactions:** Maintain detailed records of every transaction involving the escrow account, including dates, amounts, purposes, and parties involved. This documentation will be crucial for audits and client inquiries. This is also required in many states.

- **Utilize Accounting Software:** Consider using specialized accounting software designed for law firms. Many of these tools have features specifically for managing trust and escrow accounts, making it easier to track funds and generate reports.

- **Compliance with State Regulations:** Ensure that your accounting practices comply with your jurisdiction's specific regulations regarding escrow accounts. This includes adhering to any mandated reporting or auditing procedures.

- **Periodic Reviews:** Conduct periodic reviews of your escrow account records to identify any discrepancies and ensure compliance with legal requirements.

Understanding and managing escrow accounts is a fundamental aspect of legal practice for attorneys. Not only does it demonstrate professionalism and accountability, but it also safeguards client interests and helps maintain the integrity of the legal profession.

CHAPTER 7

Scaling Your Practice

> • *"Growth is never by mere chance; it is the result of forces working together."* — *James Cash Penney*

Scaling your business is an exciting but challenging stage in its lifecycle. The journey from a small, manageable operation to a thriving, larger entity comes with its share of risks and rewards.

Whether you're growing a law firm, a consulting agency, or another service-based business, scaling must be done with careful planning, strategic decision-making, and an eye on both short-term profitability and long-term sustainability.

Expanding Your Service Offerings

As your business grows, diversifying and expanding the services you offer can help you tap into new markets, meet evolving client needs, and increase revenue streams. However, expanding too quickly without proper planning can overwhelm your resources, dilute your brand, and cause operational inefficiencies. The key is to strike a balance between innovation and stability.

Identifying New Opportunities

The first step in expanding your services is identifying new opportunities. This process should be driven by both market demand and client needs. Start by analyzing your current client base and the types of services they most frequently request. Are there additional services that align with their needs that you're not yet offering?

For example, in the legal field, a solo practitioner specializing in estate planning may notice that clients often inquire about tax law or elder law services. These are natural extensions of estate planning that could be incorporated into the firm's offerings. Similarly, a business consultant focusing on marketing strategy might expand into offering digital marketing services like SEO, content creation, or social media management.

Another approach is to survey your clients directly. You can ask them what additional services they'd find helpful or what challenges they face that your business could address. This can lead to untapped opportunities for growth that you may not have previously considered.

Evaluating Your Expertise and Capacity

While it's tempting to expand services quickly, it's important to ensure that you have the expertise and capacity to deliver high-quality results. Stretching yourself or your team too thin can lead to lower service standards, which might harm your reputation. Assess whether you have the skills or if you need to hire specialized talent to introduce new services.

For example, if your law firm decides to offer immigration services in addition to family law, you'll need to evaluate whether you have attorneys with expertise in immigration law. If not, this may be the time to bring on someone with that specific skill set.

Creating New Service Packages

Once you've identified new opportunities and evaluated your capacity, consider how you'll package and market these services. Bundling complementary services into packages can be an effective way to increase sales and provide greater value to your clients.

For instance, a law firm could offer a "Family Planning Package" that includes estate planning, elder law, and healthcare directives. A marketing consultant could offer a "Digital Presence Package" that bundles SEO, social media management, and website optimization.

Offering tiered packages—basic, mid-level, and premium options—can cater to different client budgets while increasing your chances of upselling. Clients who might hesitate to pay for individual services may find value in a bundled package that addresses several needs at once.

Hiring Additional Attorneys or Staff

As your business expands, so too will the demand for more hands to help manage the workload. Hiring additional attorneys, paralegals, administrative staff, or freelancers is a crucial part of scaling, but it's not without its challenges. Bringing on the wrong person or hiring too quickly can hinder growth instead of accelerating it.

Determining When to Hire

One of the most common challenges business owners face is determining the right time to hire. You don't want to bring on extra staff too early and incur unnecessary payroll expenses, but you also don't want to wait too long and risk burning out your existing team or losing clients because you're stretched too thin.

Start by evaluating your workload and client base. If you're consistently turning down new work because you don't have the capacity or if you're constantly overwhelmed with deadlines, it's likely time to bring someone new on board. It's also important to consider the kind of tasks that are taking up most of your time. If administrative work is eating into the time you should be spending on billable tasks, hiring support staff might be the solution.

Types of Hires to Consider

When scaling your business, you have several options for the types of hires to make. It's important to assess your immediate needs and long-term goals before deciding which positions to fill.

- **Full-Time Employees:** If your workload is consistently growing and you need reliable, long-term support, hiring full-time employees can help provide stability. Full-time attorneys or staff can be trained to align with your business goals, ensuring quality and consistency.

- **Part-Time or Contract Workers:** If you're not ready to commit to full-time employees, consider hiring part-time staff or contract workers. This can be particularly useful for tasks that don't require a full-time commitment, such as bookkeeping, marketing, or specialized legal work. Contract employees offer flexibility and can be scaled up or down depending on workload.

- **Freelancers:** For project-based work, freelancers can be an excellent option. Freelancers are particularly helpful for scaling non-core functions like content creation, digital marketing, or graphic design. In legal settings, freelance attorneys may handle specific cases or projects without the need for a long-term commitment.

- **Virtual Assistants:** Many service-based businesses benefit from virtual assistants

(VAs) who can handle tasks like client communication, scheduling, and billing remotely. VAs are often a more affordable option than full-time administrative staff, and they can help free up time for more billable work.

Building a Strong Company Culture

As your team grows, company culture becomes increasingly important. Your firm or business's culture will influence everything from employee satisfaction to client experiences. A positive, collaborative culture where employees feel valued will foster higher productivity and lead to better outcomes for your clients.

Define clear expectations for your team, including performance goals, communication standards, and client service protocols. Encourage ongoing training and professional development to ensure that your staff continues to grow alongside your business.

Moreover, create an environment of open communication. Employees and contractors should feel comfortable offering feedback, asking questions, and suggesting improvements to your workflows. A strong culture promotes a sense of ownership among your team, making them more invested in the success of the business.

Building a Strong Referral Network

One of the most powerful tools for scaling a service-based business is a referral network. Referrals from satisfied clients, professional peers, and strategic partners can provide a steady stream of new business. This is especially important in competitive fields and other service industries where trust and reputation are paramount.

Leveraging Client Referrals

Your existing clients are one of your best resources for acquiring new clients. A happy client is more likely to recommend your services to others, so your first priority should always be delivering excellent results and maintaining strong relationships with your current clientele.

Encourage referrals by creating a referral program. Offering a small incentive, such as a discount on future services or a gift card, can motivate clients to refer their friends, family, or colleagues to your business. Make sure to express gratitude to those who refer new clients—acknowledging and rewarding their efforts helps build loyalty.

You should also make it easy for clients to refer others. Provide referral cards or send follow-up emails that encourage them to share your services. Additionally, online reviews and testimonials can serve as powerful social proof. Encourage satisfied clients to leave reviews on platforms like Google, Yelp, or industry-specific websites.

Forming Partnerships with Other Professionals

Another way to build your referral network is by forming strategic partnerships with other professionals. For example, if you're a business attorney, you might develop a partnership with a local accountant or financial planner. By referring clients to one another, you both benefit from increased business.

Identify complementary services that align with your business. For a law firm, this could include real estate agents, financial advisors, or business consultants. For a marketing consultant, it could be web designers, content creators, or SEO specialists.

Reach out to these professionals and propose a referral partnership. Be clear about the value you offer and how you can help their clients. Referral relationships should be mutually beneficial, so always think about how you can help others grow their businesses as well.

Networking and Community Involvement

Finally, becoming an active member of your professional community can lead to organic referral opportunities. Attend networking events, join industry associations, and participate in online forums or LinkedIn groups where your target audience and peers are present.

Community involvement is another excellent way to establish yourself as an expert in your field. Host workshops, give talks, or sponsor local events to raise your business's profile. These activities allow you to meet potential clients and partners while demonstrating your expertise.

Scaling your practice or service-based business requires a thoughtful approach to expanding your services, hiring new talent, and building a strong referral network. By identifying opportunities for growth, hiring strategically, and fostering strong relationships with both clients and professional peers, you can ensure that your business continues to thrive as it scales. With the right systems and a focus on long-term sustainability, scaling becomes not just a milestone but a catalyst for further success.

CHAPTER 8

Technology and Innovation in Legal Practice

- *"The future of the legal profession will not be defined by those who resist change, but by those who embrace technology to enhance the delivery of legal services." — Richard Susskind, Legal Technology Expert*

As I navigate the complexities of my legal practice, I've come to realize that embracing technology and innovation is not just an option; it's a necessity for survival and growth in today's fast-paced business environment. The legal industry is evolving, and to remain

competitive, we must adapt and leverage technological advancements.

In this chapter, I will share insights on how you can effectively embrace legal tech solutions, understand the transformative impact of artificial intelligence (AI) and automation, and stay ahead of industry trends. By integrating these innovations into your practice, you can streamline your

operations, enhance client experiences, and ultimately thrive in this competitive landscape.

Embracing Legal Tech Solutions

The journey toward modernization in your legal practice begins with adopting legal tech solutions. When I first explored this realm, I was amazed at the range of tools available designed to enhance efficiency and accuracy. Legal tech encompasses everything from case management software to document automation and e-discovery tools. The most significant advantage of implementing these solutions is that they minimize repetitive tasks, allowing you to focus on what truly matters— serving your clients effectively.

Selecting the right case management software is a critical first step. I cannot emphasize enough how transformative this tool can be for your practice. It helps you manage client information, track case files, and stay on top of deadlines—all in one centralized platform. For instance, I chose a case management system that integrates billing, task management, and communication tools.

This integration has significantly streamlined my workflow, enabling me to manage multiple cases with ease. Features, such as calendar synchronization and deadline reminders, are invaluable, reducing the risk of overlooking crucial dates and, consequently, minimizing potential malpractice claims.

Document automation has been another game-changer for me. Drafting legal documents can be incredibly time-consuming and prone to errors, especially when you're working with templates for contracts, pleadings, or briefs. By implementing document automation software, I can create customizable templates that allow for quick and accurate document generation. This has not only saved me countless hours but has also improved the consistency and compliance of my legal documents. I've found that incorporating electronic signatures further simplifies the process of executing documents, making it easier for clients and eliminating the need for in-person meetings.

In today's hybrid work environment, effective communication is paramount. Collaboration tools have become essential in fostering seamless communication with clients and team members. I've invested in cloud-based platforms that enable secure file sharing, video conferencing, and real-time collaboration, which have proven indispensable, especially when coordinating with remote teams. By prioritizing collaboration, I've improved my responsiveness to client inquiries and minimized time spent on mundane administrative tasks.

Of course, while we embrace these technologies, we must remain vigilant about data security and compliance. The legal profession is governed by strict privacy regulations, and the mishandling of sensitive client information can have dire consequences. Therefore, it's essential to select legal tech solutions that prioritize security—look for features like robust encryption, access controls, and secure cloud storage. Regular training for your team on data handling best practices is equally important to safeguard client information and uphold your firm's reputation.

As you embark on this technological journey, fostering a culture of innovation within your practice is crucial. Encourage your team to suggest new tools and approaches. This collaborative mindset can lead to further efficiencies and improvements in service delivery.

The Impact of AI and Automation

The advent of artificial intelligence is revolutionizing the legal landscape in ways I never thought possible. One of the most significant benefits of AI is its capability to analyze vast amounts of data swiftly and accurately. For instance, AI-powered legal research tools allow me to sift through case law and precedents in a fraction of the time it would traditionally take.

The use of AI can save so much time. By automating routine tasksI've been able to allocate my time and resources more effectively. Automation reduces the likelihood of human error, ensures consistency in processes, and frees up valuable time that I can devote to more complex legal matters. The result is a more streamlined operation that not only benefits my practice but also enhances the client experience.

However, the integration of AI and automation is not without challenges. As we increasingly rely on technology, it is essential to remain aware of potential ethical implications and the need for human oversight. AI should be viewed as a tool to enhance, not replace, the critical thinking and judgment that only a legal professional can provide. Maintaining this balance is key to ensuring that we harness the power of AI while preserving the integrity of our legal practice.

Staying ahead of industry trends is crucial in this fast-paced environment. As technology continues to advance, it's vital to remain informed about emerging tools and practices that could enhance your legal practice. Regularly attending industry conferences, participating in webinars, and engaging with legal tech communities are excellent ways to stay updated on the latest developments.

CONCLUSION

Congratulations on reaching the end of this transformative journey! You have taken a significant step toward scaling your practice into a six-figure business, armed with knowledge and strategies that can truly change the trajectory of your career. It's time to reflect on what you've learned, acknowledge your commitment, and prepare yourself for the exciting road ahead.

Recap

Throughout this book, we've explored the foundational steps necessary for building a successful practice. From establishing a solid legal foundation and conducting thorough market research to setting up your practice with the right technology and team, each chapter has equipped you with valuable insights and actionable strategies.

We've discussed the importance of effective marketing and client acquisition, emphasizing how a strong online presence and traditional strategies can propel your growth.

As we progressed, we delved into financial management, exploring various fee structures and billing practices that align with your goals. We also covered scaling your practice by expanding your service offerings and building a robust referral network. Finally, we addressed the pivotal role of technology and innovation in the legal field, guiding you on how to embrace legal tech solutions and stay ahead of industry trends. Each of these elements plays a crucial role in not just surviving but thriving in today's competitive landscape.

Now it is time to step out on faith.

The Importance of Continuous Learning and Adaptation

While you now have a comprehensive toolkit at your disposal, it's essential to remember that the legal landscape is constantly evolving. The insights and strategies you've learned are just the beginning. The importance of continuous learning and adaptation cannot be overstated. The most successful practitioners are those who remain open to new ideas, technologies, and approaches. They understand that adaptability is key to not just keeping pace with change but leading the way in their field.

I encourage you to seek out further education opportunities—be it through webinars, workshops, or industry conferences. Engage with your peers, share insights, and learn from one another. Stay informed about emerging trends and best practices in legal tech, marketing strategies, and client relations. Subscribe to newsletters that update you as the law changes. By committing to ongoing development, you will position yourself as a thought leader in your practice area, and your clients will notice your dedication to excellence.

Additional Resources and Support

As you set out on this journey, know that you are not alone. Networking is another invaluable resource; connecting with fellow professionals can provide you with mentorship, collaboration opportunities, and a wealth of shared knowledge.

Consider joining professional organizations or local bar associations that align with your practice. These groups often offer workshops, networking events, and access to valuable industry resources. Additionally, don't hesitate to seek out a business coach or mentor who specializes in helping legal practitioners scale their practices. Having someone to guide you and provide tailored support can be instrumental in navigating the complexities of running a successful business.

As you step forward, remember that every challenge is an opportunity in disguise. Embrace the journey with an open heart and an innovative spirit, and watch as your practice flourishes beyond your wildest dreams. Congratulations once again, and here's to your continued success in creating a thriving legal practice!

About the Author

Candice E. Iheme is a powerhouse. From working at a Fortune 500 insurance company to working as a litigator in an AMLaw 100 firm, rocking a judicial clerkship, interning at the state and federal level, and amassing over 600 pro bono hours before graduating law school—the list goes on! Ms. Iheme graduated *cum laude* from Rutgers University with a degree in economics and a minor in psychology. As a first-generation Nigerian-American, she was meant to succeed and make her family proud.

Fun fact, Ms. Iheme's law firm was the fifth (and most successful) business that she ever started.